Delinquency and Young Offenders

Parent, Adolescent and Child Training Skills 2
Series Editor: Martin Herbert

Delinquency and Young Offenders

by
Clive R. Hollin, Deborah Browne and
Emma J. Palmer

Series Editor
Martin Herbert

BPS Blackwell

Editorial Offices:
108 Cowley Road, Oxford OX4 1JF, UK
  Tel: +44 (0)1865 791100
350 Main Street, Malden, MA 02148-5018, USA
  Tel: +1 781 388 8250

First published 2002 by The British Psychological Society and Blackwell Publishers Ltd,
a Blackwell Publishing company

Library of Congress Cataloging-in-Publication Data

Hollin, Clive R.
    Delinquency and young offenders / Clive R. Hollin, Deborah Browne, Emma J.
Palmer.
            p. cm. — (PACTS series—Parent, adolescent and child training
skills 2)
    Includes bibliographical references.
    ISBN 1–85433–357–7 (pbk. : alk. paper)
    1. Juvenile delinquents—Services for—United States.   2. Juvenile
delinquents—Mental health—United States.   3. Social work with
youth—United States.   4. Family social work—United States.   I. Browne,
Deborah.   II. Palmer, Emma J.   III. Title.   IV. Series.
    HV9104 .H74 2002
    364.36—dc21

                                                            2002001499

A catalogue record for this title is available from the British Library.

Set in 12.5 on 13.5 Perpetua
by Ace Filmsetting Ltd, Frome, Somerset
Printed and bound in Great Britain by
TJ International, Padstow, Cornwall

For further information on
Blackwell Publishers, visit our website:
www.blackwellpublishers.co.uk

Contents

5

Delinquency and young offenders

Introduction

In thinking about the structure and contents of our contribution to Professor Herbert's Series we were mindful of several considerations. The first point to note is that the projected readership for the Series is primarily practitioners and students. The second point is that in attempting to cover the topic of delinquency we were acutely aware of the range of issues involved, meaning that any short text must necessarily be selective. Thirdly, given the need to be selective, we felt it important to communicate information about recent developments in the field. In order to try to address these three points in the best way, we have adopted an evidence-based approach to the material we present. In other words, we have looked to the recent evidence on best practice and used that as a foundation from which to discuss theory and research as it informs practice. The standpoint informing our approach is that of the scientist–practitioner: we believe that the practitioner who is informed about advances, theoretical and empirical, in their field is an effective practitioner. Thus, we have written this text with that stance uppermost in our mind. The result is, we hope, a source of information that both practitioners and students will find useful and informative in their work. We should stress that this is not intended to be a 'cook book', although we refer to ample sources for those who want to find recipes for their practice. In the field of working to reduce offending there are important gains to be made by successful practitioners: we hope that the material we present here helps towards that end. It is not our task here to be prescriptive, as we think that is inappropriate, but to try to make clear some of the principles and procedures that we believe underpin effective interventions with delinquents.

It is a fact of life that adults will complain about young people's behaviour. It is also a fact of life that, at times, there will be widespread social condemnation and moral outrage associated with the behaviour of young people. It is not difficult to find examples of adult indignation, often media-fuelled, with young people: for example, Teddy Boys, Mods and Rockers, Hippies, and Punks have all felt the weight of society's censure. There are good arguments that such teenage rebellions are almost a natural process as each generation matures and develop its own identity. As the teenage years turn to adulthood, so young people engage with society in a more responsible manner and 'grow out of crime' (Rutherford, 1986). If this 'natural process' of growing out of crime actually were the case, then it would be unnecessary to have to intervene to change child and adolescent delinquent behaviour.

The empirical evidence shows that across the adolescent population, both male and female, rates of offending slowly increase after about 8 years of age, climb to a peak at 16–17 years of age, then drop sharply at 18 years of age and beyond (Farrington, 1995). Further, most offences committed by adolescents are status offences, such as driving underage and consuming alcohol. It would be safe to state that, to use Moffitt's (1993) term, most crime committed by young people is 'adolescence limited'. However, not all young people will desist from offending: some juvenile offenders become adult offenders and continue to commit crimes beyond their adolescence. A significant contribution of the longitudinal studies into life span patterns of offending is that they have identified factors associated with longer-term offending or, as Moffitt calls it, 'life-course persistent' offending (Moffitt, 1993). These predictive factors for persistent offending include a range of social, economic and behavioural characteristics: the list encompasses general antisocial childhood behaviour such as problems at school and dishonesty and aggressiveness, high levels of impulsivity and risk-taking, poor school attainment, family criminality, periods of separation from parents, parental conflict and siblings with behaviour problems, family poverty and poor housing, and parental child-rearing behaviour characterized by harsh and authoritarian discipline and poor supervision.

There are two points to make about what is known about predictive factors. The first is that any theoretical account of juvenile offending must include a wide range of factors: the second is that when there is a cluster of these predictive factors the long-term consequences are bleak. Following the latter point, it is clear from the longitudinal research that as delinquents reach early adulthood, around 18 years of age, and become persistent offenders their lifestyle is characterized by heavy drinking, sexual promiscuity, drug use and minor crimes. Further, chronic offenders are unlikely to have gained any formal qualifications and have a work pattern of unskilled manual jobs punctuated by frequent periods of unemployment. As they grow older, by age 32 years, chronic offenders are unlikely to be home owners, they will have low-paid jobs, more family problems, including separation from their children, and are likely to have drink and drug problems. With a history of petty and violent offences, chronic offenders will have a record of fines, probation and prison sentences.

It is clear that with persistent juvenile offenders the long-term consequences are potentially serious on several levels:

1. The young person seriously involved in criminal conduct is set for a less than happy life; there is nothing glamorous about a life spent in and out of prison for petty, nasty offences.
2. Juvenile offending disrupts and destroys families, spreading harm and unhappiness.
3. As young offenders become adult criminals so the chances are that their children will, in turn, become delinquent, perpetuating the cycle of family criminality.
4. All crimes have victims and, to a greater or lesser extent, victims will suffer as a consequence of the offender's actions.
5. The public purse pays heavily for the cost of crime: if that money could be saved, so funds could be used for the greater good on services such as education, medical care, and so on.

It is evident therefore that there is a wide range of benefits to be had from preventing or reducing delinquent behaviour. The issue, of course, is how to tackle delinquency in an effective manner. It is clear from the research noted above that there is a distinctive assortment of characteristics predictive of delinquency that should set the agenda for change. However, it is also clear that change needs to be brought about on a number of levels, including the individual, the social and the economic. Given this, is there any point in working directly with the young people when such a range of other factors are involved?

Part I: What do we know about effective work to reduce delinquency?

The notion of crime prevention by working directly with offenders dates from the early 1900s and from that time a great deal of work has taken place. However, in the mid-1970s treatment for offenders became less popular, influenced by Martinson's (1974) paper titled 'What works? Questions and answers about prison reform'. Based on a review of the literature, Martinson advanced the position that, despite years of trying, 'nothing works' in changing offenders' behaviour. The view that nothing works became widely accepted by both academics and policymakers alike. It has been argued that the rejection of the concept of rehabilitation suited academic theories of crime based on political analysis; and was in keeping with the political mood of the time, with its emphasis on justice and punishment. Thus, the doctrine of nothing works suited the mood of the times, and it quickly grew from a theoretical argument to a widely accepted truth.

There was some opposition with a number of writers – most notably Paul Gendreau and Robert Ross (e.g. Gendreau & Ross, 1987) – maintaining that effective rehabilitation was possible and citing examples of successful treatment. However, one of the problems in the debate lay in making sense of a large number of research studies. In the field of offender treatment, there are different types of intervention, conducted in different settings, with different measures of 'success': it follows that it is difficult to know exactly what works, for whom, under what conditions.

Martinson had adopted the tactic of pooling the results of several hundred studies and 'vote counting': with more negative results than positive results the negative view prevailed. However, the problem with this narrative approach to making sense of the literature is that fine-grained information is lost and this can lead to faulty or imprecise conclusions.

The development of the statistical technique of *meta-analysis* has provided a means to produce a standardized overview of a large number of empirical studies. While not without its own methodological issues, it is the case that the meta-analyses have had a significant impact on current thinking in offender treatment (Hollin, 1999).

Meta-analyses: An overview

The statistical technique of meta-analysis allows a systematic review to be made of a body of evidence, in effect using the findings of each individual study as data points in a larger, comprehensive analysis. This large-scale analysis then allows precise conclusions to be drawn about the overall effects of treatment and, specifically, about what style of intervention works best in what setting.

There have been a number of meta-analyses directed at the offender treatment literature, several are widely cited (McGuire, 1995), with the study by Lipsey (1992) acknowledged as a major piece of work, involving an analysis of 443 treatment outcome studies in field of juvenile delinquency. In considering the findings of the meta-analytic studies, it is important to make the distinction between *clinical* and *criminogenic* outcome variables.

Clinical outcomes refer to a change in some dimension of personal functioning, such as psychological adjustment, cognition, anger control or skill level. Criminogenic outcomes, however, refer to measures concerned with crime, for example recidivism and type of offence. As a generalization, it is the case that programmes with a specific clinical aim tend to produce beneficial clinical outcomes. It is possible, however, that an intervention produces a significant clinical outcome, but for that clinical change to have no impact on criminogenic variables. For example, some of the research on the effectiveness of skills training with juvenile delinquents showed that while the young people become more socially competent, this had no effect on their offending. One of the benefits of the meta-analyses is that they untangle the confusion between these clinical and criminogenic outcomes.

There are now several syntheses of the meta-analyses that focus on the effects of treatment on criminogenic outcome (see McGuire, 1995). It is evident that some studies show a high treatment effect, while a considerable number of studies show either no treatment effect or even a negative effect, in line with the views of the advocates of nothing works. These syntheses have led to the development of a consensus in the literature, around the title 'What Works', regarding the elements of effective treatments to reduce offending.

Elements of successful work with delinquents

Table 1 describes the characteristics of 'What Works' programmes that show a high effect in terms of a reduction in criminal behaviour.

The meta-analyses suggest that when treatment has the characteristics

Table 1   Characteristics of high-effect interventions to reduce offending

1. Indiscriminate targeting of treatment programmes is counterproductive: an important predictor of success is that intensive work should be aimed at medium- to high-risk offenders.

2. The type of treatment programme is important, with the evidence favouring a structured and focused approach: in practice, this refers to behavioural, skill-orientated and multimodal treatments. Further, the focus of the intervention should be those areas of the young person's functioning known to be related to their offending (referred to as criminogenic need).

3. The most successful treatments, while behavioural in nature, include a cognitive component in order to focus on the attitudes and beliefs that support antisocial behaviour.

4. With respect to the type and style of service, Andrews et al. (1990) suggest that some therapeutic approaches are not suitable for general use with offenders. Specifically, they argue that 'Traditional psychodynamic and nondirective client-centered therapies are to be avoided within general samples of offenders' (p. 376).

5. Treatment programmes conducted in the community have a stronger effect on offending than treatments conducted in residential settings. For residential programmes to be consistently effective, they should be linked structurally with community-based work.

6. The most effective programmes have high 'treatment integrity' in that they are carried out by trained staff and the treatment initiators are involved in all the operational phases of the treatment programmes. In other words, there is effective management of a sound rehabilitation programme.

given in *Table 1*, then it can have a high effect, a decrease in recidivism of the order of 20 to 40 per cent over and above the baseline levels from mainstream criminal sanctioning of offenders.

Rather than 'nothing works', a position Martinson himself had withdrawn from in his later writings, it can be stated, with confidence, that rehabilitation programmes can be effective in significantly reducing recidivism.

The meta-analyses have also highlighted the importance of treatment integrity.

The importance of treatment integrity

The concept of treatment integrity is straightforward: it simply means that in practice treatment procedures are conducted correctly (Hollin, 1995). Originally developed to assist those in training as psychodynamic psychotherapists, high treatment integrity means that practitioners follow the theoretically correct principles and procedures. To achieve high levels of integrity there is a need to train practitioners to high levels of treatment competence. However, in order to ensure that integrity is maintained, there is the need for supervisory and management structures that facilitate the work of practitioners and monitor and evaluate the design, implementation and progress of treatment (Hollin et al., 1995).

As the meta-analyses clearly indicate that a cognitive–behavioural approach is advantageous in working with offenders with the goal of reducing recidivism: it follows that integrity procedures would be directed towards this end. In terms of cognitive–behavioural treatment techniques, there are a number of publications available that cover this substantial field of antisocial behaviour in young people (e.g. Goldstein et al., 1998; Hollin & Howells, 1996). Briefly, cognitive–behavioural theory explains behaviour in terms of the individual interacting with his or her social world. As they encompass and exemplify the 'What Works' principles, the focus here is on two key aspects of the delinquent's social world. The first is work with the family as the agent of the young person's socialization. The second is treatment with a focus on the way in which the young person thinks of him or herself in relation to his or her world, generally referred to as social cognition.

Part II: Families and delinquency

It has been understood for some time that the family can have a role in accounting for a young person's delinquent conduct. The research in this area has highlighted the nature and role of family factors in explanations of delinquency, allowing effective interventions to be conducted.

Family factors and delinquent behaviour

A profusion of studies has shown that adults and young people who engage in criminal behaviour have often been exposed to dysfunctional or unstable family lives during their formative years. Indeed, as noted above Farrington (1995) included factors related to family functioning – including siblings with behaviour problems, family poverty, poor parental child-rearing behaviour, parental conflict and separation from parents when the child is aged 8 to 10 years – as among the most important independent predictors of later delinquency. It is important to develop an understanding of how these factors influence delinquency if preventative measures are to be successful.

Although family factors are frequently described in terms of sociological and sociodemographic characteristics, they can be divided into two basic types with reference to psychological processes:

1. It is supposed that the child learns behaviours through modelling, child-rearing practices and dysfunctional relationships within the family.
2. The emphasis is on the development of child psychopathology because of problems with attachments and parent–child relationships.

The factors underpinning these processes are not mutually exclusive: familial influences regarding juvenile delinquency are probably a mixture of both processes.

Parental criminality

Farrington et al. (1996) showed that the conviction of one family member was strongly related to convictions of every other family member. This relationship appeared to be particularly strong between an offending father and a son whose offending persisted into adulthood. There is substantial evidence that parental criminality has a strong association with the development of criminal behaviour.

Given this strong link, many theorists have concluded that genetic factors must play a role in the development of an antisocial personality. This position has been supported by twin and adoptee studies that attempt to separate environmental and genetic effects. It would appear, however, that the evidence for hereditability appears to be strongest when antisocial behaviour is linked to hyperactivity and to antisocial behaviour that persists to adulthood. In the case of adolescent-limited antisocial behaviour and delinquency the genetic influence appears to be weaker.

Wright (1994) proposed another explanation for this pattern of findings. He described how Darwinism explained criminal behaviour in terms of an adaptation to the environment. Children's moral development, or 'conscience', is shaped by their encounters with their immediate environment from a very early age. Evolutionary theorists propose that genes programme how the mind adapts to fit the context, rather than programming behaviour itself. Delinquents then, can be seen as victims of society rather than victims of their genes.

There is evidence of a cyclical pattern of violence that is probably not a direct result of genetic factors. For example, children who grow up in families where their parents are substance misusing tend often to develop their own drug and alcohol problems, as well as to engage in delinquent and aggressive behaviours. Similarly, children who have been treated harshly themselves tend to have problems forming stable and nonviolent relationships with other adults. It could be argued that children learn to be antisocial by modelling the antisocial behaviour of their parents. Additionally, as shall be discussed in more detail later, relationships between children and parents may be damaged to such an extent that the child's ability to deal with other people also becomes dysfunctional.

Sibling factors

Several studies have shown that the presence of a delinquent sibling increases the risk of delinquency. If there were a genetic basis to delinquency, then this would not be surprising. As noted, however, the influence of genetic factors on juvenile crime is probably quite low, indicating that environmental factors must also play a role. Generally speaking children from the same family will be exposed to similar, if not identical, risk factors, both within the family and in their immediate environment. In this way it follows that siblings will share experiences of parenting, poverty, disruption, and perhaps abuse and neglect. The sibling influence has also been explained in terms of large family size, as discussed later. It may be the case that the risk of delinquent behaviour is high for all children from families who display the critical risk factors, and that there is little reason to expect that siblings of a delinquent young person will not themselves engage in delinquent behaviour. Alternatively, it has been suggested that delinquent siblings transmit their behaviour to other children in the family, probably through a modelling effect. This suggestion is substantiated by the fact that the sibling influence is strongest in cases where the young person is most open to influence, as when the delinquent sibling is older or of the same sex. If this corruption is indeed the case, it needs to be considered how best to limit the influence that a delinquent sibling has over his or her brothers and sisters.

Parenting skills

Unfortunately parenting skills are not instinctive and not all parents have developed a finely tuned ability to distinguish adequate from poor parental practice. Various studies have shown that the experience of poor parenting is associated with the development of antisocial behaviours. An American study reported by Jackson and Foshee (1998) showed a relationship between *responsive* parenting (defined as how well the parent responded to the child when needed) and *demanding* parenting (how much the parent was inclined to have rules and expectations in regard to the child's behaviour) and violent behaviour in adolescents. The more responsive and demanding the parents were, the less likely it was that the young person engaged in antisocial behaviour with their peers. Young people who rated their parents lower on these dimensions, however, were more likely to engage in violent behaviours such as hitting peers, bringing a weapon to school or threatening a peer with a weapon.

In general, the literature indicates that parents of delinquents:

➢ fail to monitor their children;
➢ neglect to reward and encourage prosocial behaviours;
➢ do not respond positively to children's needs;
➢ fail to distinguish between their own mood state and the child's behaviour;

> ➤ give ambiguous and conflicting feedback;
> ➤ do not handle crises and problem-solving effectively;
> ➤ fail to set clear standards; and
> ➤ use harsh and erratic discipline.

When parents display these characteristics, then it *is* possible to teach them new skills. This will be discussed in more detail in a later section, and the types of skills that can be taught are described in *Appendices I* and *II*. Severely poor parenting comes under the heading of *child abuse and neglect* and is discussed later.

Winnicott (1956) theorized that delinquency is actually a healthy reaction to poor parenting and inadequate supervision. He felt that the normal child develops the capacity to control his or her own behaviour when helped by a stable home environment. The child's parents help by monitoring the behaviour and appropriately disciplining the child. When parents do not succeed in this role, the child has not learned what behaviour is appropriate and what is not appropriate. The uncontrolled child therefore looks for control outside the home. According to this model, then, antisocial behaviour is the child *externalizing* a need for strong parenting.

Another view, however, is that children from deprived backgrounds *internalize* their representations of the world. Theorists who propose this view, such as John Bowlby, argued that infants develop an internal working representation, or *schema*, of their primary caregivers, based on their mutual interactions. The child develops expectations about how their caregiver will respond to a situation and will try to predict what will happen. Eventually this schema is generalized to the world at large. Children who have been cared for by inadequate or abusive parents form schematic representations of the world as a harsh and hostile environment. These children are more likely to react to the world in an antisocial manner. This is because they interpret ambiguous interpersonal cues as threatening and hostile and, accordingly, respond to meet (perceived) aggression with aggression. This information-processing model is discussed in more detail later.

Attachment

Attachment theorists, such as John Bowlby and Mary Ainsworth, hold that many adult psychopathologies, including the development of delinquent behaviour, are due to the failure of infants and small children to develop secure attachments to a primary caregiver. Bowlby (1953) originally emphasized the impact of maternal deprivation above all else, basing many of his early claims on a comparison study of juvenile thieves and a matched control group. In this study, Bowlby found that the juvenile thieves were far more likely to have experienced complete separation from their mothers for six months or more in the first five years of their lives. Bowlby concluded that early maternal deprivation was related to antisocial behaviour, and that a child needs to establish a relationship with his or her mother in early life. Later studies, however, indicated that separation from the mother did not necessarily have this impact, particularly when the child could become attached to a caring and warm individual.

There is more recent evidence to suggest that the attachment patterns of infants and their early relationships with their mother *do* influence later cognitive and social development. Securely attached children have been found to:

➤ be more cognitively competent;
➤ show more social proficiency;
➤ get along better with their peers; and
➤ be less likely to develop emotional or behavioural problems.

It has also been theorized that adult attachment patterns are influenced by early experiences. Indeed, research suggests that there are adult attachment styles that roughly correspond to the infant attachment patterns. Anxious and insecure attachment patterns have been found to predict problems in the child's later development, and 'Pattern D' (disorganized and disoriented) infants appear to be especially at risk for developing aggressive and antisocial behaviour problems. Hirschi (1969) theorized that attachment to significant others was, for males, 'Conducive to the development of conventional attitudes, forming a bond between the juvenile and society, hence preventing delinquency' (p. 27).

In cases of extreme parental neglect, the child may be deprived of any opportunity to form a selective attachment. Such deprived children may suffer from Reactive Attachment Disorder, often called anaclitic depression. They fail to respond to the normal social stimuli, tend to withhold close bodily contact, and have difficulties forming relationships later in life. The relationship between troubled attachments and psychopathology is supported by evidence from animal research. Harlow's classic work with rhesus monkeys, for instance, showed that infant monkeys brought up without a parent or substitute attachment figure had dramatically troubled social relationships (e.g. Griffin & Harlow, 1966).

Broken homes

The issue of whether children from broken homes, such as those with divorced or separated parents, are at increased risk for delinquency is a controversial one. There is evidence to suggest that divorce has lasting repercussions into adulthood, with children from divorced parents:

➤ entering into sexual relations earlier;
➤ making poor occupational choices;
➤ developing less stable long-term relationships;
➤ developing long-term problem behaviours; and
➤ suffering from depression and other anxieties.

Indeed, the relationship between delinquency and broken homes has been repeatedly highlighted.

Alternatively, however, it needs to be considered whether these problems are really the result of parental separation, or whether other factors play a role. Block et al. (1986) reported data from a prospective study of 101 children, 41 of whom had divorced parents. The findings indicated that the children, especially boys, from divorced parents had already shown signs of personality disturbance years before their parents divorced. Block et al. concluded that the problems that divorced children develop might well be due to the atmosphere of conflict that exists during their formative years. In support of this conclusion, further research showed that when children move from a home where there was a lot of conflict to a more stable environment, then their problems tended to diminish. This finding would indicate that marital or family conflict is possibly more predictive of delinquency than is the breaking up of a family. This position is further substantiated by an indication that an increase in antisocial behaviour following parental death is minimal.

Single-parent families

It has been found that children raised in single-parent families are more likely to display antisocial behaviour. In the past, poverty and poor parenting have traditionally been blamed for the link between single-parent families and delinquent children. It has been suggested, however, that such a link cannot be the full explanation: too many people are choosing to have families and remain unmarried, regardless of their financial status. It follows that other factors may play a role: for example, Rankin and Kern (1994) found that children living in single-parent families, who were strongly attached to their custodial parent, were more likely to commit delinquent acts than children living in intact homes who were strongly attached to *both* their parents. Their study also indicated, however, that children from intact homes who were strongly attached to just one of their parents were more likely to commit delinquent acts. This would reinforce the view that warm attachments, but particularly multiple attachments, act as a protective factor against delinquency.

Large family size

A number of studies have indicated that delinquents tend to come from large families (Farrington, 1995). There are several possible reasons for this family size effect. As noted, having a delinquent sibling increases the risk of delinquency, possibly through a modelling effect. The more siblings that are present, the greater the chance that a young person will have been exposed to delinquent behaviour. Parents of children in large families may also find it more difficult to monitor and supervise their children, and to respond appropriately to different behaviours. This type of low-level parenting has been associated with delinquency.

Another possible explanation is that larger families may have less economic resources, so the type of stress and conflict associated with poverty (see next section) comes into play. If this is the case, interpersonal relationships are compromised because of the increased stress and conflict of living with so many people. In support of this view, it has been suggested that large family size did not predict delinquency if living conditions were less crowded. In a similar vein, it has also been suggested that children do not get the opportunity to form close attachments with their parents when they are members of larger families. As has already been described, close attachments appear to act as a protective factor against delinquency (Hirschi, 1969).

Poverty and economic deprivation

Children who have experienced early socioeconomic hardship have been found to display aggressive and antisocial behaviours later in life, and to be less popular than other children among their peers. It is difficult to separate the simple fact of being poor from other risk factors for delinquency, such as large family size, single-parent families or broken homes. It would appear, however, that economic pressure does influence parental stress, depression and marital conflict. These strains in turn influence parent–child and

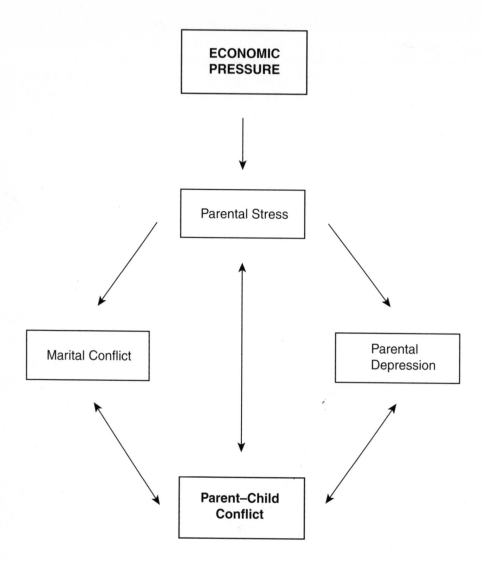

Figure A   Economic deprivation and family relationships

parent–adolescent relationships, which eventually leads to antisocial behaviour by the young person. As *Figure A* illustrates, the effect of economic stresses has a two-way impact on family relationships, which only serves to threaten each dyadic relationship (i.e. mother–child; father–child; mother–father) even further.

Figure A highlights the two-way relationship between the secondary stressors in this pattern and familial conflict. Economic pressure causes parental stress, which may result in conflict between the adults in the family, with the possible consequence of parental mental illness such as depression. Increased stress, conflict and the cognitive distortions caused by depression are all likely to increase parent–child conflict. This family conflict (itself a consequence of stress) is, in itself, likely to become an additional stressor, and may further exacerbate the levels of parental stress, marital conflict and depression. The family situation is then caught in a continuing spiral of deterioration. As described above, the conflict and damaged relationships that may eventually result from living in a stressful family environment has an impact on how the young person deals with their wider environment. It has been shown that both marital conflict and parent–child relationships can affect the coping abilities of young people. It has also been suggested that an extremely discordant situation such as poverty may bring about a 'maladaptive emergency response' such as delinquency.

Familial abuse and delinquency

Defining abuse

The relationship between familial abuse and delinquency is complex. Beside the fact that child abuse may occur in the presence of other risk factors for delinquency, there are problems inherent in determining the long-term individual consequences for victims of child abuse. Over the years many researchers have found it difficult to find an appropriate and comprehensive definition of child abuse. Definitions tend to depend on the perspective from which the issue is being approached, and the individual researcher's personal and professional experience. The matter is further complicated when the abuse is familial: traditionally parents have been allowed more leniency with regard to what constitutes reasonable chastisement. Regardless, certain acts or omissions by the child's caretaker, such as those that endanger life, can be seen as clearly inappropriate and damaging. However, distinguishing the exact nature of damage to the child is complicated by the different forms that abuse can take: different types of abuse have been shown to be associated with distinct effects on children.

Within a family, a child may be subject to:

- physical abuse;
- sexual abuse;
- verbal abuse;
- emotional abuse;
- long-term neglect and deprivation (e.g. physical, emotional, educational, moral);

> witnessing the abuse of other family members;
> witnessing violence and destruction of property; and
> repeat and multiple victimization.

Although many researchers and practitioners may look for the effects of one type of abuse or another, it is inherently difficult to separate the effects of different forms of child abuse and neglect. It is likely, for instance, that physical abuse is accompanied by harsh verbal chastisement, and that many physically abused children will witness other forms of domestic violence. Unfortunately many children are victimized on several occasions, a pattern which may be repeated in adulthood. Finally, of course, it is often difficult to determine which children are victims of abuse. Indeed, perhaps because of fear or embarrassment, abuse may go undetected for years or even a lifetime.

Physical punishment as reasonable chastisement

The first question to be asked relates specifically to physical punishment: when does corporal punishment become physical abuse? In the UK, as in many other countries, parents have legally and morally been allowed considerable latitude to self-determine what constitutes reasonable chastisement or punishment for their own children. Indeed, large numbers of parents consider that physical punishment is reasonable chastisement, with 80 to 90 per cent of parents in the UK and the USA using a 'mild slap' on occasion. It appears that mothers and fathers are equally likely to use physical punishment with the same frequency.

Given that harsh forms of discipline have been associated with the development of delinquent behaviour, there has been concern about using milder forms of corporal punishment. There is some indication in the literature that physically disciplining a child is likely to have a damaging influence, with the ensuing conclusion that all corporal punishment is potentially abusive. Strassberg et al. (1994), for instance, found that the stronger the form of physical punishment (rated 'Non-users', 'Spankers' and 'Violent'), the more aggressively the child would behave. The children of 'Non-users' displayed the lowest levels of aggression, indicating that even milder physical punishment (spanking) increases maladjustment in the child. There is also an argument that using physical force against children, even in a relatively mild form, may be damaging to the child's self-esteem and to parent–child relationships. The effects of physical chastisement may be exacerbated when corporal punishment is used against an adolescent, whose physical size means that the amount of force considered necessary to subdue him or her is considerable. Furthermore, it is suspected that physical punishment follows a cyclical pattern across generations, with those who have been slapped or beaten as a child more likely to themselves use violence against their children.

The evidence against the use of physical punishment is not unequivocal, however, as research has also shown that there are other variables that need to be considered. There is some evidence that found that parental involvement was a better indicator than harsh physical punishment of child or adolescent maladjustment. Findings like this show that it is not absolutely clear whether or not slapping influences the development of antisocial and delinquent behaviours. Nonetheless, there is sufficient evidence to warrant concern about the frequent use of physical punishment. For example, should the evidence suggest that mild slapping is not harmful, what constitutes a 'mild' slap is a subjective definition that will vary between families and between individuals. It has been suggested that, in many cases, abuse is merely an extension of punitive parenting styles.

Child abuse and delinquency

Despite the difficulties of defining abuse and distinguishing its parameters, it is still necessary to attempt to isolate the effects of child abuse. Various researchers claim to have found evidence of an association between diverse emotional and behavioural problems and different types of child abuse (e.g. Iwaniec, 1995), including the child being a witness to domestic violence and marital conflict. It may be considered debatable to refer to the latter (witnessing domestic disharmony) as abuse, but as Cummings (1997) stated 'Exposure to highly negative expressions of marital conflict, at the least, is a significant source of adversity that contributes to children's risk for the development of psychopathology' (p. 6). Indeed, Jaffe et al.(1986) found that boys who witnessed violence had similar levels of emotional and behavioural problems to boys who had been physically abused.

Being a witness to acts of *domestic violence* has been associated with:

➢ conduct disorders and other externalizing behaviours;
➢ aggressive behaviours;
➢ lower levels of self-control;
➢ depression;
➢ poor social problem-solving skills;
➢ post-traumatic stress disorder; and
➢ psychological problems as children.

In the same way, there is a catalogue of the effects of *physical abuse*, such that it has been associated with:

➢ antisocial or disruptive behaviour;
➢ aggressive behaviours;
➢ low self-control;
➢ truancy;
➢ insecure attachment; and
➢ Reactive Attachment Disorder.

Again, the effects of *sexual abuse* are such that children subjected to this form of abuse have been found to display:

➢ antisocial or disruptive behaviour;
➢ aggressive behaviours;
➢ sexually risk-taking behaviours;
➢ substance abuse;
➢ truancy;
➢ guilt;
➢ low self-esteem; and
➢ post-traumatic stress disorder.

Finally, it has been demonstrated that *emotionally abused and neglected* children may show:

➢ aggressive and disruptive behaviours in school;
➢ self-harming behaviour;
➢ lack of social skills;
➢ low self-esteem;
➢ insecure attachment; and
➢ nonorganic failure-to-thrive/Reactive Attachment Disorder.

Some of the above effects of abuse can be described as secondary, rather than direct, influences on delinquency. These secondary effects of abuse, such as low self-esteem, poor social skills and insecure attachment, are symptoms of abnormal developmental patterns. They show that the child or young person has not developed a capacity to cope effectively with social situations. In many cases this developmental delay is manifest in externalizing and antisocial behaviours, although some responses appear to be internalized, especially in the case of emotionally abused and neglected children.

Hughes (1997) noted 'Abnormal attachment patterns may be the most devastating effect of abuse and neglect on the child's development' (p. 25).

Indeed, it has also been postulated that very often a lack of infant–caregiver bonding precedes maltreatment (Iwaniec, 1995). Either way, disturbing reactions to early deprivation and maltreatment can be seen in children who display anxious attachment patterns and, in extreme cases, symptoms of Reactive Attachment Disorder, as described in a previous section. Although evidence suggests that abused children may retain the ability to modify their attachment behaviour if their situation improves, very often this means that the child must be taken from the family environment for this to be a possibility. While foster and residential care may help some of these children, it is also possible that alternative care may only further complicate the situation for many other children and young people.

Foster families and delinquency

When a child's family situation deteriorates to a certain condition (although the exact nature of this condition is subjective and somewhat arbitrary), the child is taken into the care of the state. Over the past few decades foster care has become by far the more preferred form of alterative care for children experiencing family problems. Institutional care has been shown to result in negative behaviours such as aggression, and poorer functioning as an adult. Although it is the more appropriate choice for most children, foster care is not without its own problems.

Over the years many studies on children in foster care have found a high incidence of criminal and antisocial behaviours: indeed, the incidence of antisocial behaviours tends to be higher in foster care than in the general population. The levels of antisocial behaviour can become severe, as seen in stealing, truancy and unwanted sexual advances. Foster parents are often ill-equipped to deal with the aggressive and difficult behaviours they encounter, and will generally ask for such children to be removed from their care. Thompson et al. (1994) noted that, notwithstanding elaborate training and preparation, many foster parents found the behaviours of their sexually abused foster children too 'bothersome' to continue the placement. Special projects have been set up just to deal with these young people who are otherwise deemed 'unfosterable'. These projects are not as widely available in the UK as they probably should be and many children and young people who display severe behaviour problems continue to drift through the care system for years. Instability of care is, unfortunately, frequently a prelude to entering prison as criminal activity escalates through adolescence and into adulthood. Quinton et al. (1986), for example, found that 22 per cent of the women in their sample who had been in care had criminal records, compared to none of the control group.

Why do foster children engage in delinquent behaviours?

When researchers theorize about why foster children develop a propensity for criminal behaviour, the temptation is to look no further than the factors that have been repeatedly shown to be associated with the development of these behaviours. Generally, then, the usual reasons for delinquency are offered:

➢   maternal deprivation;
➢   a history of abuse;
➢   poverty;
➢   being born into a criminal subculture;
➢   exposure to a dysfunctional or unstable family environment; and
➢   erratic parenting.

Indeed, many foster children have experienced some or several of these problems, and it is generally accepted that they do play a role in delinquent behaviour in foster children. Thompson et al. (1994), for instance, were able to isolate behaviours that appeared to occur more frequently in sexually abused children. The possibility that disruptive behaviours may develop or deteriorate *as a consequence* of being in care, however, has not been examined extensively.

There are two possible ways in which foster care may contribute to the development of criminal behaviours that cannot be blamed entirely on the child's past experiences. The first is simply that most fostering programmes fail adequately to address the problems that these children bring with them in to care. In addition to the experiences that took them from their homes in the first place, these children must deal with all of the identity, stigma and attachment issues that have been reported to follow placement in community care. Most foster parents do not receive adequate training and preparation to help them deal with issues that might come up during the placement. As with normal parenting, parents with specific parenting skills are found to cope better with the demands of foster parenting. Foster parenting is *not* normal parenting, however, and it is not appropriate to expect low-skilled and ill-prepared couples to be able to deal effectively with a vulnerable and potentially antisocial young person unless they are offered appropriate and long-term training and support. It is hardly surprising that so many placements break down because foster parents find they are ill-equipped to deal with both the child's behaviour and the effect of this behaviour on their family. When the limits of the foster parents' tolerance are reached, the child is asked to leave the family home whereupon the placement is said to be a 'breakdown', or more euphemistically a 'disruption'.

The next failing of the fostering system lies in how children are treated after the breakdown of a placement. Foster care is, by its very nature, a substitute arrangement, and such instability is not conducive to sound child-rearing practices. For some children, however, even their substitute families become replaced when placements end prematurely. Researchers have found that the experience of multiple placements is common in foster children, and having experience of a previous breakdown further decreases the chances of success in later placements. Past placements in both foster and residential care have been found to have an impact on the development of antisocial and problem behaviours but, again, children are rarely given adequate support to help them cope with these moves.

Foster children are frequently deprived of the opportunity to form lasting and positive attachments. It has been found that the older a child is when she or he is placed with a foster family, the more likely it is that problems will develop. At this point attachments, however anxious or disorganized, have already been formed to the natural family or to the previous carers. This previous experience complicates the demands of fostering to develop a new bond with a new family. It has been shown that carefully planned psychotherapy with these children will eventually allow them to form positive attachments again (Hughes, 1997), but unfortunately their emotional insecurity is not always given the attention it deserves, both before and after the foster placement.

Working with parents and children

Working with families generally takes two major forms, namely prevention and treatment. Preventative programmes have been set up to improve the parenting skills of parents from at-risk groups, to teach foster parents to deal with specific issues that they encounter and to help improve the social skills of children and young people. Treatment programmes work with comparable groups, but often with an emphasis on dealing with what *has* happened rather than what *might* happen. One such example is Trauma-Specific Therapy for sexually abused children, which emphasizes treating the effects of the abuse. Various psychodynamic approaches to therapy have also been found to be very useful in changing the behaviour of children who have been exposed to damaging influences. Many of these programmes are limited only to certain family members: treatment programmes for domestic violence, for example, have typically focussed on the adult victim or the offender, and not child witnesses. While the interventions discussed in this section may be used both as preventative and therapeutic strategies, the emphasis is on how working with families should be used to prevent antisocial and criminal behaviours in children and young people.

Teaching parenting skills

Although poor parenting and child abuse and neglect have been repeatedly associated with the development of delinquent behaviour, little systematic work has addressed this issue. Any parent knows from experience that babies do not come with a user's guide!: how then can poorly skilled, often young, people be expected to behave in an effective manner when they become parents? As Iwaniec (1995) pointed out:

> Parent-training is perhaps a major development in helping parents to become better equipped to understand their children's developmental needs and better informed to deal with child-rearing problems as the occur. Strangely enough, and in spite of the recognition of world-wide serious child-rearing and child-management problems, little has been done to educate people and prepare them for parenthood. (p. 137)

The programmes that have attempted to deal with this issue by training parents to use effective parenting skills have met with some degree of success (Webster-Stratton & Herbert, 1994). Many of these programmes base their methods on social learning theory or cognitive–behavioural and behaviour therapy techniques. Through competent use of methods such as videotape modelling, film, role-play, group discussion and effective supervision and support, parents are taught the skills necessary for more effective parenting. Examples of the type of effective parenting skills that parents can be taught are outlined in *Appendix I*.

Parenting skills such as positive reinforcement, limit-setting and effective problem-solving have been shown to be valuable in many family situations, including when the child has a conduct disorder. It is important to remember, however, that some situations require different skills. It has been pointed out, for instance, that parenting an adolescent is very different to parenting a younger child. The boundaries between intrusiveness and monitoring are less defined, and an adolescent is likely to respond with far less deference to attempts to restrict behaviour. Parents of adolescents may find it more appropriate to modify their parenting. They can do this by respecting the growing need for autonomy while maintaining positive communication with the young person. Guidelines on the type of skills that are appropriate here are outlined in *Appendix II*.

Personal and interpersonal skills

Problem-solving skills

Ineffective problem-solving skills have been associated with dysfunctional families, marital conflict, poor parenting and other factors frequently associated with delinquency. Teaching parents to solve common problems more adaptively can help to reduce both marital conflict and parent–child conflict. These problem-solving skills can help the adult to respond more appropriately to a potential conflict situation, and may mean a change in the parents' own cognitions. Programmes that address problem-solving deficits aim to:

➢ improve constructive communication between family members;
➢ help parents to generate more solutions to child-rearing and marital problems, so that they learn to choose less aggressive strategies;
➢ restructure their cognitive representations so that the parent's perception of his or her child's or partner's behaviour is not distorted; and
➢ identify the most common conflict situations and attempt to alter how they are dealt with.

Problem-solving techniques have also been used to help children deal with aggression. The child is taught to deal with social problems by first generating and examining possible solutions. After analysing various fictional problems and planning effective solutions, the child is encouraged to apply these skills to real-life situations.

Coping skills

The association between family, and indeed other social factors, and delinquency is generally only manifest after repeated exposure to particular environments and to particular experiences. The young person may be coping as effectively as he or she can with their environment. What actually constitutes effective (also called adaptive or productive) coping, however, is very hard to define: not only may it differ from person to person, but it may also vary depending on the circumstance (Frydenberg, 1997). For instance, a young person may respond to bullying by becoming aggressive in return. If this strategy results in a cessation of bullying then it could be argued that the young person coped effectively with the stressor. In such a case they identified the problem, assessed possible solutions and acted effectively on their assessment. Alternatively, however, it could also be argued that the young person responded in a manner that shows poor emotional management, which is indicative of a more dysfunctional manner of coping. In this particular example, the context leaves room for some ambiguity of interpretation. However, if the same young person responds aggressively to a nonconfrontational social situation, then it is more evident that she or he does not cope adaptively with social stresses.

It has been suggested that maladaptive coping in adolescence is the result of two factors: (a) a deficit in the young person's perceptual representation of what is happening; and (b) a deficit in coping resources. These two deficits are probably brought about by repeated exposure to certain circumstances. Indeed, research indicates that how effectively a young person copes depends on how stressful his or her life experiences have been, and the strength of their family relationships. If delinquent behaviour is a manifestation of maladaptive coping, then the development of adaptive coping strategies may well be a protective factor for delinquency.

As Frydenberg (1997) commented: 'It is possible to transform non-productive coping into productive coping. The instructor, counsellor or clinician can create the environment where young people become aware of their coping and focus on developing their coping skills' (p. 177). She claimed there were three prerequisites for conscious development of coping skills: these three prerequisites are *self-awareness, motivation to change* and the *necessary skills* (e.g. positive self-concept, positive outlook) to achieve the desired outcomes.

Frydenberg (1997) postulated that coping abilities could be enhanced through both self-help techniques and professional support. The first self-help technique she described is *Optimism*, which may involve re-educating how the young person views events. She also advocates the use of *Humour*, to help the young person relax and cope more effectively. Finally she recommends the young person uses *Metaphor* to help describe how they cope. Some metaphors represent more deficient coping mechanisms than others, and the individual should be encouraged to change these internal representations to more adaptive ones. By learning to use more adaptive coping mechanisms, it is argued, young people will be better able to resist the situations that lead to criminal activity. *Appendix III* summarizes the factors, with reference to the material discussed here, that are necessary to help promote productive coping strategies in young people.

In summary, it is clear that a great many economic, social and family factors must be taken into consideration in both understanding delinquency and designing effective intervention programmes to reduce juvenile offending. However, it would be unwise to neglect the individual in the situation –

individual interaction that leads to delinquent behaviour. In the final section the emphasis moves to a consideration of those individual factors, with a particular note of the effect that recent research is having on both theory and practice.

Part III: Advances in working with delinquents

Delinquency is a social act committed in a social context, it follows that a complete account of delinquency must include the individual's thoughts on the situation. This aspect of delinquency is captured in the study of social cognition.

The role of social cognition in delinquency

Before the role of social cognition in delinquency can be explored, it is necessary first to consider the question 'what is social cognition?'. This is not a straightforward question to answer as social cognition is a broad term, encapsulating several facets of the individual's social functioning. However, a useful working definition is to take social cognition as the capacity to understand other people and to be able to solve problems in social situations.

Thus, this definition includes the ability to interpret accurately a social situation and to be able to respond to its demands in an appropriate way. Various cognitive skills are needed for this process to take place, such as the ability to stop and think before acting, to see matters from other people's view point (perspective–taking), taking responsibility for one's own actions and the consequences arising from these, and to be able to solve social problems by identifying the most appropriate course of action.

The early research that examined these social cognitive skills was diverse in nature, although a number of researchers concentrated on the differences between offenders and nonoffenders. A review of this research by Ross and Fabiano (1985) revealed a number of patterns or styles of cognitions which appear to characterize offenders. These aspects of the cognitive functioning of delinquents are summarized below:

➤ *Self-control/impulsivity*: offenders tend to show a failure to stop and think about all the possible options for action and their consequences.

➢ *Concrete reasoning*: offenders' thoughts may be action-oriented, rather than reflective and abstract.

➢ *External locus of control*: offenders tend to attribute events to external forces such as luck or other people, rather than to their own internal control.

➢ *Empathy/social perspective taking*: offenders often show a lack of ability to see situations from others' point of view.

➢ *Egocentric*: this aspect of cognition is related to social perspective-taking and refers to offenders' tendency to think the world revolves around themselves.

➢ *Social problem solving*: offenders tend to have an inability to weigh up situations accurately, to generate possible solutions, consider the consequences of their actions and formulate plans to reach their desired outcomes.

➢ *Moral reasoning*: offenders tend to have less mature moral reasoning than nonoffenders, and be more concerned with costs/benefits of behaviour than its impact on relationships or society.

However, it is important to state that individual differences dictate that not all offenders will show all (or, indeed, any) of these patterns of social cognition.

Social information-processing model

The initial research into the role of social cognition in delinquency during the 1970s and early 1980s was scattered, with little attempt made to pull the findings together into a coherent theoretical model. The early research also tended to concentrate on the patterns of cognitive skills, and neglected the process of how they were linked. This state of affairs changed when Kenneth Dodge and his colleagues constructed a six-stage model describing how individuals take in social information and process it in social situations (Crick & Dodge, 1994):

1. the encoding of social cues about the situation from the environment;
2. the interpretation and mental representation of the situation using social cues and internal schema;
3. clarification of goals for the situation;
4. access of possible responses for the situation;
5. decision about the response for the situation; and
6. enactment of the chosen response.

While these stages are seen as being sequential, there are also feedback loops between the stages.

At the first stage, individuals attend to various situational social cues, encode these at a cognitive level, and then use them to interpret the situation. Research has found that some types of cues are better remembered than others, with more recent cues (i.e. those at the end of an interaction) and more salient cues (i.e. those that have more personal significance to the individual) being recalled with a greater level of accuracy.

The individual's interpretation of the situation at the second stage of the model involves making a personal mental representation of the situation: this includes the making of attributions about the intent of other people in the situation and the causes of events. As well as using the information gathered from social cues, information from past experience is used in the form of social schema and scripts. These memory structures, formed from prior social experiences, give rise to 'working models' of the world that influence how individuals perceive, organize and remember social information.

At the third stage, a goal or desired outcome for the specific situation is chosen. Individuals bring their own personal goal orientations and motivations to social situations and this, along with circumstantial factors such as emotional state, influence the choice of goals. Once a goal has been set, possible responses are explored. These goals may either be newly constructed in response to the needs of the situation or accessed from memory. In order to choose the response to act upon, the possibilities of different courses of action are evaluated in terms of various factors, including the probable outcome, their perceived efficacy, the likelihood of success in terms of achieving the goals identified at stage 3, their appropriateness and ease of execution. Finally, the chosen response is enacted.

At each stage, information from memory will influence how new information is processed and, in turn, new events and experiences will be assimilated into this database of memories, resulting in changes or revisions. Therefore, it is possible to see how past experience plays a role in determining people's behaviour through contributing to their 'model' of the world.

Social information processing and delinquency

Research has consistently shown that there are distinct patterns of social information processing and cognitive distortions associated with antisocial behaviour and delinquency in children and adolescents. This research will be summarized below, but for more detailed reviews see Crick and Dodge (1994) and Palmer (2000).

Attention and representation

Looking first at the initial two stages of Dodge's model, the individual forms mental representations (or *schema*) of the situation based on encoded situational cues and from previous knowledge of similar situations. Although using previous knowledge, in the form of schema, to help interpret a situation can be effective as a 'cognitive short-cut', overreliance on schema can lead to vital social cues being ignored in a given situation. Research has demonstrated that aggressive children do tend to collect less situational information before they interpret a situation. Similarly, aggressive children pay more attention to aggressive social cues than to nonaggressive cues. This pattern of findings is supported by research showing aggressive children to have a greater tendency to rely on internal schema in interpreting situations and, where social cues were used, to concentrate on those from the end of the interaction (i.e. a recency effect). Therefore, the overall picture is one where aggressive children show selective attention to and recall of cues, along with an overreliance on internal schema to interpret social situations.

Aggressive children also have a tendency to show a low level of accuracy when attributing intent and causality in social situations, with an overemphasis on the attribution of hostility on the part of other people: a phenomenon known as hostile attributional bias. This relationship between antisocial behaviour and a hostile attributional bias has been found in many studies of children and adolescents.

Social goals

At the third stage in Dodge's model, behaviour has been found to be associated with the types of social goals an individual deems to be important. Goals that enhance relationships are associated with prosocial behaviour and positive social adjustment. Conversely, goals that are likely to damage relationships are associated with aggressive and antisocial behaviour. This point is reflected in research showing that aggressive children and adolescents typically select goals where the motivation for their actions is revenge and domination.

Generating responses

With respect to the fourth stage of the model, generation of responses, there are three points at which aggressive and antisocial children may differ from their peers: (a) the number of responses generated; (b) the content of these responses; and (c) the order in which responses are accessed. Aggressive and antisocial children and adolescents generate significantly fewer responses to social situations than their nonaggressive peers. This finding indicates that these young people may have a limited repertoire of responses from which to choose, or that they have problems in generating new responses when needed. There are also differences in the content of responses, with aggressive children's responses being more aggressive and less prosocial. Even when aggressive children do manage to access an initial response that is nonaggressive and appropriate, subsequent responses are still likely to be aggressive.

Evaluating possible responses

When it comes to evaluating responses, aggressive children and adolescents tend to rate aggressive responses positively and competent responses negatively, with the opposite pattern found among their nonaggressive peers. This may be due to the fact that aggressive children have more positive outcome expectations for aggressive responses than they do for competent or prosocial ones, and that aggressive children feel more comfortable using aggression than other responses.

Social skills

Finally, even once a response has been chosen, an individual needs to have the required social skills to enact it. The outcome of choosing and acting upon a particular response also impacts on future choices. If a response is successful in terms of achieving the desired goals or outcomes for the situation, it will be positively evaluated and be more likely to be used in the future. However, a response that is perceived to be unsuccessful or difficult to enact is unlikely to be chosen again.

Having established the nature of social information processing in aggressive and antisocial children and adolescents and in their nonaggressive peers, research has turned to the factors involved in how patterns of cognition are acquired and maintained. The establishment of the patterns described above have been seen in young children, which suggests that they are acquired at a young age. At a young age, parents and caregivers are the primary influence on children, leading research to concentrate on the link between social information processing patterns and child-rearing practices. This research has begun to elaborate on the association between the impact of early experiences, behaviour and social information processing. An early harsh, unloving environment is likely to lead the child to form cognitions in the form of hostile schema, and social scripts that construct a view of the world as a hostile place. In a given situation this view may lead to a hostile response being evoked due to the easy access to these hostile schemas and scripts. In turn, the child's behaviour may elicit reactions from other people that corroborate the child's perception of the world as a hostile place (i.e. they are punished for their actions). If this chain of events continues unchecked, aggressive behaviour can escalate and may eventually become delinquent behaviour.

Therefore, referring to the social cognitive skills listed at the start of this section, it is possible to see how most of these fit into Crick and Dodge's (1994) model. The one that remains, however, is moral reasoning, as this is more concerned with the content of social cognition rather than the processes. The study of the relationship between moral functioning and delinquency has developed significantly over the recent years.

Moral maturity and delinquent behaviour

Most people would agree that a person's behaviour is related in some way to their thinking and reasoning. It follows that people's moral actions or behaviour are related to their moral reasoning, suggesting that different behaviours and actions are the result of different reasoning processes.

Three specific issues have been raised when trying to explain the relationship between thought and action as it relates to moral cognition (sometimes called moral reasoning) and moral behaviour:

➢ people's knowledge of what is right and wrong, i.e. the laws and morals of a society;
➢ people's attitudes to these laws and morals; and
➢ the reasoning and criteria by which decisions about moral behaviours are justified.

However, psychological research has found little relationship between people's knowledge of what is right and wrong and their behaviour. As everyday experience tells us, people acquire basic knowledge about what is right and wrong as they grow up, but a considerable number of people still break the law and commit acts that they know are wrong. ·

Similarly, there is a lack of evidence for a strong relationship between people's attitudes to laws and morals and their actual behaviour. This may appear surprising at first, but there are a number of personal and situational factors that may influence an individual's decision about whether or not to act in a certain way. For example, other attitudes and motives may interfere with a particular decision; while the presence of other people can influence decision making, as seen in the force of peer pressure on delinquent behaviour. In terms of moral reasoning and delinquency, the research primarily concentrated on how people reason about moral issues, and how decisions are reached as to what actions to take in a given situation.

Kohlberg's theory of moral reasoning

Lawrence Kohlberg (1969) proposed a six-stage theory of moral reasoning, whereby people's moral reasoning changes as they mature and grow older. These six stages are split into three levels, each containing two stages: the three levels are first *pre-conventional*, followed by *conventional*, and finally *post-conventional*. These labels refer to the way in which people reason about moral issues and justify behaviour. Overall, the progression through the stages is seen as moving from a view of the world and rules as fixed and external to a person (known as concrete reasoning), to an appreciation that these rules are more flexible, reciprocal and result from cooperation (known as abstract reasoning). Kohlberg proposed that as people mature, they move through the six stages, from stage one to stage six, in sequence, although not everyone reaches the highest stages. Furthermore, at any point in time, a person may reason from more than one stage, although these are commonly adjoining ones. This is due to the fact that people do not jump from one stage to the next, but move gradually from one stage to the next, as their intellectual capabilities increase.

The details of Kohlberg's stages of moral reasoning are shown in *Table 2*.

Longitudinal and cross-sectional research evaluating Kohlberg's theory of moral reasoning supports the content and progression of the moral stages. Cross-cultural work has found similar developmental patterns in several countries, although in nonindustrialized cultures progression tends to be slower. As the research found very few people reached the final stages of moral reasoning, Kohlberg later revised his theory without stage 6.

Moral reasoning and offending

Kohlberg's theory has also been applied to offending behaviour, and it is proposed that at different moral stages people will justify breaking the law in different ways and for different reasons:

Table 2   Stages in Kohlberg's theory

Level 1: Pre-conventional reasoning
At this level the individual has little or no understanding of societal rules and
regulations. Moral reasoning is determined by selfish considerations and conformity
to the rules of authority. Rules are seen as external to the person.

Stage 1: Moral reasoning is determined by avoiding punishment and obedience to
          perceived authority figures.
Stage 2: Moral reasoning is hedonistic, with consideration only for the person's own
          needs based on the balance of rewards and punishment.

Level 2: Conventional reasoning
At this level the person realizes the reciprocal nature of rules, and decisions about
behaviour are made on the basis of maintaining social contracts.

Stage 3: Individual becomes aware of the needs of other, with relationships becom-
          ing the most important factor in moral reasoning.
Stage 4: Moral reasoning becomes concerned with maintaining society's rules and
          laws for the sake of upholding society itself.

Level 3: Post-conventional reasoning
At this level the person understands that society's rules are based on underlying
moral principles.

Stage 5: Individual perceives that society's law are a contract between themselves
          and society. However, under certain circumstances laws can be broken.
Stage 6: Moral reasoning is determined by self-chosen ethical principles, and these
          may overrule society's laws when they conflict.

➢ Stage 1   Breaking the law is justified if punishment can be avoided.
➢ Stage 2   Breaking the law is justified if the gains/rewards outweigh
               the risks/costs.
➢ Stage 3   Breaking the law is justified if it helps to maintain relation-
               ships.
➢ Stage 4   Breaking the law is justified if it helps to maintain society,
               or is sanctioned by societal institutions.
➢ Stage 5/6   Breaking the law is justified if it maintains basic human
               rights or furthers social justice.

From the different circumstances in which an individual might judge it
justifiable to break the law, it is likely that those at the lower stages will be
more frequently encountered. It follows, therefore, that the theory predicts

that those who offend will be more likely to be reasoning at lower moral stages than those who do not offend.

This prediction has been tested many times by psychologists in the last 30 years, typically studying convicted offenders, and using self-reported delinquency checklists with different offender groups. The consensus from the reviews is that the evidence supports the prediction: offenders tend to show less mature moral functioning than those who do not commit offences.

The next issue to address is that of a potential mechanism for the link between moral reasoning and delinquency. Three possible explanations have been offered, which also raise a number of unanswered questions with respect to Kohlberg's theory.

First, delinquents' moral reasoning level may be a product of a subculture (e.g. a gang), rather than the highest possible level they are capable of using. This possibility was raised by Kohlberg himself, although it appears to lack empirical support.

Second, it has been suggested that family background may mediate the relationship between moral reasoning and delinquency. This possibility is supported by research showing that delinquents tend to come from disadvantaged backgrounds (Farrington, 1995) and that moral reasoning is associated with parental rearing.

Third, it may be the case that the moral immaturity among delinquents is a result of retrospective justification of their behaviour, although this area has not been empirically explored in any depth.

Working with cognition

Having identified a number of areas where social cognition is related to delinquency, it should be possible to develop interventions that aim to address these issues and ultimately reduce offending behaviour. For example, if a young person's immature moral reasoning is thought to be implicated in their offending behaviour, then it might be considered worthwhile offering an intervention that concentrates on raising their moral reasoning level.

There are a number of interventions that have developed in response to the needs of delinquents' social cognitive functioning: these will be considered here under the subheadings of social skills training; cognitive–behavioural programmes; and multimodal programmes.

Social skills training

The original social skills model outlined by Argyle and Kendon (1967)

contained three components. First, *social perception*, the ability to understand social cues given by other people. Second, *social cognition* which refers
to the processing of information, selecting of goals, generation of responses
and decisions about responses (not unlike the Crick and Dodge model previously discussed). Finally, *social performance*, the ability to perform a social
response competently and appropriately.

Social skills training, therefore, aims to address problems associated with
all three and to increase the competence of individuals across different social
situations. This involves the teaching of both microskills related to nonverbal behaviour, e.g. being able accurately to interpret cues of body lan-
guage and eye contact; and the macroskills needed in a situation as a whole,
e.g. how to manage different situations with different people. These social
skills are typically taught through a variety of techniques, including role-
play, modelling and group discussions. Feedback and social reinforcement
is continuously provided by the trainer and by other group members. See
Appendices IV, V and *VI* for details on how social skills may be assessed and the
techniques used in social skills training.

There are many examples of social skills training interventions with delinquents, many of which include evaluations of effectiveness (for a review
see Hollin & Palmer, 2001). Interventions that concentrate on the microskills
tend to lead to an improvement in those skills taught, although the outcome
for macroskills interventions is less clear. Longer-term evaluations that examine rates of reoffending also show mixed results. Overall it would appear
that targeted social skills training is effective at changing specific behaviours,
but less so in reducing problem behaviour as a whole or reoffending.

Cognitive–behavioural programmes

Cognitive–behavioural programmes work from the principles of social learning theory and cognitive theory, and so concentrate on reducing delinquency
by changing the delinquent's cognition and behaviour. The focus, therefore,
will include both the content of cognition and its processes. Influenced by
the meta-analyses discussed previously, this style of intervention is currently
very popular with practitioners working with offenders. Several of the most
common techniques in this type of work are considered below.

Social problem-solving skills training

Social problem-solving programmes aim to address processing deficits of
the sort discussed above in relation to Crick and Dodge's (1994) model.

The training typically covers a variety of topics in order to help delinquents become more effective with dealing with social situations (see *Appendix VII* for details). The important point to raise in this type of work is how thoughts and associated actions will impact on other people.

Like social skills training, social problem-solving interventions use a variety of methods with which to teach the skills, typically including:

➤ modelling;
➤ self-instructional training; and
➤ role-play.

One issue that can be problematic if treatment is delivered in an institutional setting lies in replicating the types of social situations that young people typically experience. Further, many delinquents only show deficits in certain situations: for example, they may only experience problems when interacting with authority figures, and show few difficulties when interacting with friends. An awareness of this diversity is needed when situations for role-plays are developed.

Evaluations of social problem-solving interventions have shown positive results with respect to both social problem-solving and reoffending.

Moral reasoning development

Following the research that has shown delinquents generally to be reasoning at the lower levels of moral reasoning, a number of interventions have been developed to raise levels of moral reasoning. These interventions fall into two types, *macrointerventions* and *microinterventions*.

Macrointerventions refer to programmes that set up 'Just Communities' whereby the members have an active role in the setting and enforcing of rules. Given the practicalities of this type of intervention, these communities are often found in institutional settings, and tend to be implemented with adult offenders rather than juveniles.

The more common approach with juveniles is taken at the micro level. In this approach, moral reasoning is the focus of a groupwork programme, either on its own or in combination with another topic. In these programmes offenders are encouraged to discuss moral dilemmas in order to stimulate their moral development.

These group interventions have been evaluated, with positive changes demonstrated in treatment groups, although it is not always known if there was any corresponding behavioural change. One study that did find both moral reasoning and behavioural improvement was an intervention with delinquents in a school setting (Arbuthnot & Gordon, 1986). Further, the gains at post-treatment were maintained at a one-year follow-up.

Anger management

Anger management programmes are another common cognitive–behavioural intervention with delinquents who show highly aggressive behaviour. This particular intervention aims to give the young person the skills to manage their anger and aggression primarily through increasing their self-control. One of the most influential programmes in this area was developed by Raymond Novaco (Novaco & Welsh, 1989) and involves three stages (see *Appendix VIII* for more details):

> *Cognitive preparation*: at this stage the individual is encouraged to analyse their anger so they can recognize its causes and consequences.
> *Skill acquisition*: at this stage coping strategies to deal with anger are learned.
> *Application training*: at this stage the skills learned at the previous one are practised using role-play situations.

A similar intervention with young people that also uses the theoretical basis outlined by Novaco is Anger Control Training (Goldstein et al., 1998). This is outlined in *Appendix IX*. Interventions using these techniques have been used in both England and America, with positive impacts on anger and aggression in both community and institutional settings.

Multimodal programmes

More recently, interventions with young offenders have begun to incorporate more than one of the approaches mentioned above. This shift in emphasis is in response to the fact that many delinquents have difficulties in more than one area of their lives, and so it might be expected that targeting all of these will be more effective than concentrating on just one area. A good example of this multimodal approach is seen with the Aggression Replacement Training (ART) programme (Goldstein et al., 1998). Aimed primarily at aggressive young people, ART contains three components (see *Appendix X* for more details):

> *Skill streaming*: teaching prosocial skills through modelling, role-play and feedback.

➤ *Anger control training*: as outlined above.
➤ *Moral reasoning training*: enhancement of moral reasoning through discussions of moral dilemmas.

Evaluations of ART have been undertaken in community and residential settings and the results have indicated cognitive and behavioural improvements in treatment groups that, importantly, are maintained over time (Goldstein et al., 1998).

A second type of multimodal approach has concentrated on the content of cognitions and the distortions in these typically shown by delinquents (e.g. hostile attributions). Central to this category of interventions is the creation of a group 'climate for change'. An example of such an intervention is the Positive Peer Culture (PPC) programme (Vorrath & Brendtro, 1985), in which young people are encouraged to talk about their problematic behaviours, identify their cognitive distortions, and so challenge them in a constructive manner. The reason for a group setting is the hope that the young people involved will take responsibility for their actions and the consequences it has for both themselves and other people. Evaluations of PPC have not been as positive as for other interventions in terms of reoffending, although participating in such programmes appears to make young people more motivated to participate in further interventions.

A more ambitious intervention is the Equipping Peers to Help One Another programme (Gibbs et al., 1995), which incorporates the ART programme outlined above with the principles of PPC. EQUIP is a 10-week programme that simultaneously addresses anger management, social skills, moral reasoning and cognitive distortions in a group setting that is positive and caring. More details are given in *Appendix XI*. EQUIP has also demonstrated some encouraging results in evaluation studies, with evidence that as well as improving cognition, it also has a long-term impact on institutional misconduct and reoffending after release.

Linking advances in treatment to 'what works'

Having considered the interventions that have arisen in response to the research on delinquency, it can be seen that some approaches appear to be more effective than others at reducing offending behaviour. It is noticeable that over time interventions have become more complex, with the advent of multimodal programmes that simultaneously target more than one aspect of the young offender's functioning. Treatments have also become more successful at changing cognitions, behaviour and reducing reoffending. A great deal of this progress is due to the findings of meta-analyses which have highlighted those factors common to successful interventions (McGuire, 1995). The principles for successful intervention lie in developing structured and focused interventions that address the attitudes, values and beliefs that support delinquency. The potential impact of this type of structured programme, preferably designed in a multimodal format, is a clear message to emerge from the meta-analyses. It is also clear from the evaluation literature that interventions, such as ART and EQUIP, that follow these principles are among the most successful in reducing delinquency.

A final issue to be considered in interventions is their setting. Programmes for delinquents are found in a number of settings, ranging from closed and highly secure institutions such as Young Offender Institutions, to less secure residential settings, and in the community. The meta-analyses indicate that community interventions tend to be successful, probably because tackling problems in a natural environment allows easier transfer of new skills to real-life situations. Community-based interventions also allow other issues to be addressed, such as family problems. As many of the social and cognitive issues considered here are linked to early experiences, including child rearing, a holistic approach to interventions that takes into account how these behaviours were acquired is important.

Institutional settings for young offenders often run cognitive–behavioural programmes, although the service provided does vary across institutions. There are other concerns that need to be taken into consideration in this setting, including security and the ever-present tendency to punish. These issues can also influence the priority which rehabilitative interventions are assigned within an institution. An alternative to closed institutions is residential settings where there is less emphasis on security and punishment. This setting can allow more flexibility of treatment and links with the community to be maintained.

In summary, this final section has outlined the types of social cognitive functioning commonly found among delinquents, both in terms of the content of their cognitions and the processing of social information. From this base it has proved possible to develop and evaluate interventions aimed at changing thought and action. This development of practice has been achieved with varying degrees of success over the years, with the more recent interventions that have incorporated the results of meta-analyses being the most successful. However, young offenders are not a homogenous group, and so they will not all function in an identical manner. This fact highlights the importance of the basic treatment skill of assessing delinquents in order to target interventions accurately. Most importantly of all, if changes are to be maintained over time, then emphasis must be given to work in the community. A community emphasis has the twin advantage of facilitating the generalization of new skills, and allowing offence-focused interventions to be coordinated with those that address other problem areas in delinquents' lives.

Part IV: Concluding thoughts

It is clear that there are grounds for optimism in working with young people to reduce offending. If delinquency is a phenomenon that demands a complex, multidisciplinary, explanation then, equally, attempts at treatment must be complex and not restricted by narrow professional boundaries. In research, there is a continuing need for research with contributions from, among others, criminology, law, medicine and psychology. Similarly, in practice there is more than ever a pressing need for professionals, including police, probation workers, prison staff, medics, social workers and psychologists, to work together constructively and effectively. The current optimism and the potential benefits of effective work with delinquents should not be allowed to flounder on narrow academic or professional divisions.

References

Andrews, D. A., Zinger, I., Hoge, R. D., Bonta, J., Gendreau, P., & Cullen, F.T. (1990). Does correctional treatment work? A clinically relevant and informed meta-analysis. *Criminology, 28,* 369–404.

Arbuthnot, J., & Gordon, D. A. (1986). Behavioral and cognitive effects of a moral reasoning development intervention for high-risk behavior-disordered adolescents. *Journal of Consulting and Clinical Psychology,* 54, 208–16.

Argyle, M., & Kendon, A. (1967). The experimental analysis of social performance. In L. Berkowitz (ed.), *Advances in Experimental Social Psychology,* Vol. 3. New York: Academic Press.

Block, J. H., Block, J., & Gjerde P. F. (1986). The personality of children prior to divorce: A prospective study. *Child Development,* 57, 827–40.

Bowlby, J. (1953). Some pathological processes set in train by early mother-child separation. *Journal of Mental Science,* 99, 265–72.

Crick, N. R., & Dodge, K. A. (1994). A review and reformulation of social information-processing mechanisms in children's social adjustment. *Psychological Bulletin,* 115, 74-101.

Cummings, E. M. (1997). Marital conflict, abuse, and adversity in the family and child adjustment: A developmental psychopathology perspective. In D. A. Wolfe, R. J. McMahon, & R. D. Peters (Eds.), *Child Abuse: New Directions in Prevention and Treatment across the Lifespan.* Thousand Oaks, CA: Sage.

Farrington, D. P. (1995). The development of offending and antisocial behaviour from childhood: Key findings from the Cambridge Study in Delinquent Development. *Journal of Child Psychology and Psychiatry,* 36, 929–64.

Farrington, D. P., Barnes, G. C., & Lambert, S. (1996). The concentration of offending in families. *Legal and Criminological Psychology,* 1, 47–63.

Frydenberg, E. (1997). *Adolescent Coping: Theoretical and Research Perspectives.* London: Routledge.

Gendreau, P., & Ross, R. R. (1987). Revivification of rehabilitation: Evidence from the 1980s. *Justice Quarterly,* 4, 349–408.

Gibbs, J. C., Potter, G. B., & Goldstein, A. P. (1995). *The EQUIP Program: Teaching Youth to Think and Act Responsibly through a Peer-Helping Approach.* Champaign, IL: Research Press.

Goldstein, A. P., Glick, B., & Gibbs, J. C. (1998). *Aggression Replacement Training: A comprehensive intervention for aggressive youth* (rev. edn). Champaign, IL: Research Press.

Griffin, G. A., & Harlow, H. F. (1966). Effects of three months of total social deprivation on social adjustment and learning in the rhesus monkey. *Child Development,* 37, 533–48.

Hirschi, T. (1969). *Causes of Delinquency.* Berkeley, CA: University of California Press.

Hollin, C. R. (1995). The meaning and implications of 'programme integrity'. In J. McGuire (ed.), *What Works: Reducing reoffending.* Chichester: Wiley.

Hollin, C. R. (1999). Treatment programmes for offenders: Meta-analysis, 'what works', and beyond. *International Journal of Law and Psychiatry,* 22, 361–72.

Hollin, C. R., Epps, K. J., & Kendrick, D. J. (1995). *Managing Behavioural Treatment: Policy and Practice with Delinquent Adolescents.* London: Routledge.

Hollin, C. R., & Howells, K. (eds) (1996). *Clinical Approaches to Working with Young Offenders.* Chichester: Wiley.

Hollin, C. R., & Palmer, E. J. (2001). Skills training. In C. R. Hollin (ed.), *Handbook of Offender Assessment and Treatment.* Chichester: Wiley.

Hughes, D. A. (1997). *Facilitating Developmental Attachment. The Road to Emotional Recovery and Behavioural Change in Foster and Adopted Children.* New Jersey: Jason Aronson Inc.

Iwaniec, D. (1995). *The Emotionally Abused and Neglected Child.* Chichester: Wiley.

Jaffe, P., Wolfe, D. A., Wilson, S., & Zak, L. (1986). Emotional and physical health problems of battered women. *Canadian Journal of Psychiatry,* 31, 625–29.

Jackson, C., & Foshee, V. (1998). Violence-related behaviors of adolescents: Relations with responsive and demanding parenting. *Journal of Adolescent Research, 13,* 343–59.

Kohlberg, L. (1969). Stage and sequence: The cognitive-developmental approach to socialization. In D. Goslin (ed.), *Handbook of Socialization Theory and Research.* New York: Rand McNally.

Lipsey, M. W. (1992). Juvenile delinquency treatment: A meta-analytic inquiry into the variability of effects. In D. Cook, H. Cooper, D. S. Cordray, H. Hartmann, L. V. Hedges, R. J. Light, T. A. Louis, & F. Mosteller (eds.), *Meta-analysis for Explanation: A Casebook*. New York: Russell Sage Foundation.

Martinson, R. (1974). What works? Questions and answers about prison reform. *The Public Interest, 35*, 22–54.

McGuire, J. (ed.). (1995). *What Works: Reducing Reoffending*. Chichester: Wiley.

Moffit, T. E. (1993). Adolescence-limited and life-course persistent antisocial behavior: A developmental taxonomy. *Psychological Review, 100*, 674–701.

Novaco, R. W., & Welsh, W. N. (1989). Anger disturbances: Cognitive mediation and clinical prescriptions. In K. Howells & C. R. Hollin (eds.), *Clinical Approaches to Violence*. Chichester: Wiley.

Palmer, E. J. (2000). Perceptions of parenting, social cognition, and delinquency. *Clinical Psychology and Psychotherapy, 7*, 303–09.

Quinton, D., Rutter, M., & Liddle, C. (1986). Institutional rearing, parenting difficulties and marital support. In S. Chess & A. Thomas (eds.), *Annual Progress in Child Psychiatry and Child Development*. New York: Brunner/ Mazel.

Rankin, J. H., & Kern, R. (1994). Parental attachments and delinquency. *Criminology, 32*, 495–515.

Ross, R. R., & Fabiano, E. A. (1985). *Time to Think: A Cognitive Model of Delinquency Prevention and Offender Rehabilitation*. Johnson City, TN: Institute of Social Sciences and Arts.

Rutherford, A. (1986). *Growing Out of Crime: Society and Young People in Trouble*. Harmondsworth: Penguin.

Strassberg, Z., Dodge, K. A., Pettit, G. S., & Bates, J. E. (1994). Spanking in the home and children's subsequent aggression towards kindergarten peers. *Development and Psychopathology, 6*, 445–61.

Thompson, R. W., Authier, K., & Ruma, P. (1994). Behavior problems of sexually abused children in foster care: A preliminary study. *Journal of Child Sexual Abuse, 3*, 79–91.

Vorrath, H. H., & Brendtro, L. K. (1985). *Positive Peer Culture*. (2nd edn). New York: Aldine.

Webster-Stratton, C., & Herbert, M. (1994). *Troubled Families: Problem Children*. Chichester: Wiley.

Winnicott, D. W. (1956). *Deprivation and Delinquency*. New York: Routledge.

Wright, R. (1994). *The Moral Animal: Evolutionary Psychology and Everyday Life*. London: Abacus.

Appendix I: Guidelines to teaching effective parenting skills

In parent-skills training some of the more widely taught skills include:

➤ Identifying the current *parenting styles* used by the parents and explaining why these may not be effective.

➤ Teaching parents to use *nonphysical punishment* in a reasonable manner when discipline is required. One such technique that has been used involves invoking a penalty or cost when the child responds in a certain way (Webster-Stratton & Herbert, 1994). Parents are encouraged to come up with appropriate sanctions for undesired behaviour.

➤ Introducing the concepts of *positive and negative reinforcement* as more appropriate methods of shaping a child's behaviour.

➤ Using *praise* and affection to reward prosocial behaviour.

➤ Explaining the idea of *differential attention*. Parents are taught to provide consistent positive attention to prosocial behaviours, while ignoring inappropriate responses. This is referred to as the *'praise-ignore' formula* (Webster-Stratton & Herbert, 1994, p. 175).

➤ Teaching the importance of *setting clear limits* of acceptable behaviour. Parents are asked to question how necessary, understandable and fair their rules are, and to decide on a specific outcome if rules are not adhered to by the child.

➤ Explaining the concepts of *modelling and imitation*. Because parents of antisocial children may not have themselves learned prosocial behaviours, it is important that they are given an opportunity to observe another person performing desired behaviours at this point.

➤ Helping the parent to recognize when their reaction to the child is based on a *cognitive distortion* of what is happening rather than the actual severity of the child's behaviour.

➤ Developing *problem-solving skills*, which include helping the parent to become more sensitive to the types of social situation from which difficulties may arise, and developing an ability to generate a wider range of potential solutions to a problem.

➤ Encouraging the use of *'Time Out'* as an effective sanction to antisocial behaviour. In this procedure, the child's undesired behaviour is followed by a period where the child is excluded from a reinforcing activity or opportunity.

➤ Occasionally the use of *contracts* is discussed. Family members sit down and negotiate a written agreement between the child and the parents, stating how the parents would like the child to behave, and how the child would like his/her parents to modify their behaviour.

Appendix II: Guidelines for parents of teenagers

When a young person reaches adolescence parents need to adapt their parenting style. They can learn to do this by:

➤ Using more democratic and inductive styles of discipline. Young people who are no longer prepared to accept ambiguous or autocratic rules may accept an explanation that demonstrates the parent's perspective.

➤ Realizing that adolescents often use conflictual dialogue as a means of defining their individuality, and responding to this appropriately.

➤ Realizing that the balance of power within the family will inevitably change. It is important for adults to waive some of the authority that may have served them well when their son or daughter was younger. Parents need to learn to be more flexible and to find more age-appropriate ways of interacting with the young person.

➤ Respecting the privacy of the young person, while continuing to monitor their activities in an unobtrusive manner.

➤ Keeping open positive channels of communication.

➤ Trying to compensate for the sense of powerlessness that the young person may feel during exchanges with adults. It is important that the adolescent does not perceive his or her position to be too impotent, as this may affect the quality of communication.

Appendix III: Checklist of factors necessary to promote adaptive coping strategies in young people

1. Has the young person developed a sufficient self-awareness to consciously consider his or her behaviour in social situations?
2. Is the young person able to describe what social situations she or he considers stressful or threatening?
3. Is the young person able to describe his or her behaviour in stressful situations?

_____

Self-awareness skills

4. Is the young person motivated to change his or her behaviour in stressful situations?
5. Has the young person attempted to use more adaptive strategies to deal with stress?

_____

Motivation to change skills

6. Has the young person developed a more positive self-image?
7. Has the young person attempted to enhance his or her interpersonal skills?
8. Has the young person developed the ability to change his or her perception of stress-inducing social situations?

_____

Social and personal skills

9. Does the young person try to look at social situations in a more positive way?

_____

Optimism

10. Can the young person be persuaded to see the funny side of situations that may otherwise lead to maladaptive coping?

_____

Humour

11. Has the young person developed the ability to describe an internal concept (or metaphor) that represents how she or he copes?
12. Can the young person represent his or her coping as a positive metaphor?

_____

Metaphor

_____

Appendix IV: Checklist of social skills

➤ Ability to perceive social cues (verbal and nonverbal)?
➤ Accurate perception of social cues?
➤ Social cues used appropriately in interpreting situation?
➤ Appropriateness of goals for social situations?
➤ Knowledge of alternative responses?
➤ Quality of alternative responses?
➤ Selection of appropriate response?
➤ Consequences of response perceived?
➤ Performance levels of social skills?
➤ Situation-specific, person-specific or general problems?

Appendix V: Social skills assessment

Assessment of social skills allows problem areas to be identified and a baseline against which progress can be monitored. Assessments can be carried out in a variety of ways, including:

> - self-report checklists – plus the inclusion of a rating scale to indicate severity of problems;
> - use of diary to record behaviour and/or problems encountered; and
> - naturalistic observation in a planned setting (e.g. in a pre-intervention session).

Appendix VI: Social skills training techniques

- ➢ Modelling
  - ➢ use a number of examples per demonstration;
  - ➢ use situations relevant to the young person;
  - ➢ use situations that result in a positive outcome for the main protagonist; and
  - ➢ make the model as similar as possible to the young person.
- ➢ Role playing
  - ➢ if young person leaves role, stop and remind them of role;
  - ➢ if necessary stop and restart role play from the beginning;
  - ➢ use situations relevant to the young person;
  - ➢ feedback and contingent reinforcement;
  - ➢ give young person feedback on their performance;
  - ➢ praise for doing well;
  - ➢ praise in line with quality of performance;
  - ➢ feedback on improvements from previous sessions; and
  - ➢ reinforce wanted behaviours with praise, but NOT unwanted behaviours, i.e. make rewards contingent upon behaviour.

It may be worth drawing up a 'behaviour contract' with the young person, signed by both the worker and the young person. These outline the plan of action, schedule and goals to be achieved, and have been successful in a number of settings in getting young people to attend and complete interventions.

Appendix X: Aggression replacement training (ART)

ART addresses anger and aggression in young people through three coordinated strands:

1. Skillstreaming: Teaching of prosocial skills through modelling, role-play and feedback:
   - examples of prosocial behavioural skills needed by the young person are shown (modelling);
   - role-playing allows an opportunity for guided practice of skills;
   - feedback is given on role-playing performance and the young person should be reinforced for good performances; and
   - homework tasks are given to allow the young person to practise skills in natural setting. This should then be discussed at the next session.
2. Anger control training: Training to control and reduce anger and aggression. This is based on the ACT programme outlined previously, and focuses on:
   - identifying internal and external triggers of anger;
   - identifying personal cues that accompany anger (feelings, physiological sensations);
   - techniques to reduce anger and arousal;
   - techniques to defuse internal triggers;
   - use of appropriate alternative strategies for anger-inducing situations; and
   - self-evaluation of previous steps and their outcomes.
3. Moral reasoning training: Enhancement of moral reasoning through discussions of moral dilemmas in small group meetings. This involves four phases:
   - introduction of a situation that poses a moral problem and establishment of ground rules for discussion;

Appendix VII: Social problem-solving training

Various topics are covered under social problem-solving, all of which aim to help the young person to stop and think before acting, so that a full assessment can be made of the situation and suitable responses considered, rather than reacting in the first way that springs to mind. This approach might also include 'means-end thinking', in order to teach delinquents to think through the steps required to respond to situations so as to achieve a desired consequence.

- Problem definition – encourage the young person to accurately define the problem in specific terms before attempting to solve it.
- Generation of alternative solutions – encourage the young person to brainstorm as many solutions as possible.
- Decision making – examine all the possible solutions carefully, considering the consequences of them from a variety of perspectives before choosing the best possible solution. Consideration should be given to:
  - long-term and short-term consequences;
  - consequences on self and others; and
  - positive and negative consequences.
- Means-end thinking – once a solution has been chosen, the young person should be encouraged to plan how they will enact it effectively.
- Follow-up – once a solution has been chosen and carried out, the young person should be encouraged to check that it solves the problem satisfactorily. If it does not, they should be encouraged to identify why, and to try another solution.

Appendix VIII: Anger management techniques

Novaco's three-stage model of anger management:

1. Cognitive preparation:
   - identification of external (situational or social) and internal (personal) triggers for anger;
   - identification of how person feels when they become angry (e.g. pounding heart, adrenalin rush) so they can recognize when they are becoming angry; and
   - identification of the consequences on anger, both themselves and on other people.
2. Skill acquisition:
   - strategies to cope with feeling angry are learned. These include deep breathing, counting backwards and the use of mental imagery to calm down.
3. Application training:
   - the strategies and skills learned at the previous stage are rehearsed using modelling, role play, performance feedback and homework tasks.

Appendix IX: Anger control training (ACT)

ACT involves five steps to help control anger:

1. identification of both external and internal triggers for anger;
2. identification of the external and internal cues that indicate the individual is angry;
3. use of reminders to encourage the individual to calm down (e.g. self-talk);
4. use of reducing techniques to lower anger levels (e.g. breathing exercises, thinking about the potential consequences); and
5. self-evaluation of how well the anger was controlled and self-praise when successful.

➤ cultivation of a tone of mature morality within the group by the group leader through questioning group member's responses to elicit mature reasoning. Once elicited write on blackboard for group discussion;

➤ addressing moral developmental delay within the group by moving the focus to immature responses. Challenge these responses, write any justifications on board, and encourage other members of the group to join discussion (particularly those with mature reasoning). The aim of this stage is to shift those with immature reasoning to agreeing with those with mature reasoning; and

➤ consolidate mature moral reasoning by encouraging a group consensus on the problem situation initially outlined. The aim of this stage is that the mature morality position becomes the consensus (or at least the majority position).

The Anger Replacement Training (ART) programme is available in the following book which includes outlines of the sessions and checklists and problem situations: Goldstein, A. P., Glick, B., & Gibbs, J. C. (1998). *Aggression Replacement Training: A Comprehensive Intervention for Aggressive Youth* (rev. edn). Champaign, IL: Research Press.

Appendix XI: Equipping peers to help one another (EQUIP)

The EQUIP programme incorporates the Anger Replacement Training (ART) programme with the principles of Positive Peer Culture (PPC). It is designed to be delivered for three hours a week for 10 weeks. Before starting the EQUIP programme it is necessary to run Mutual Help Groups for 2–4 weeks in order to establish the positive peer culture.

Establishing a PPC

Mutual Help meetings are adult guided but youth run. They should be run five days a week for 1–1½ hours, although once the EQUIP programme is introduced this can drop to three times a week. It is recommended that groups contain no more than nine individuals, and if possible a group should contain people with a variety of experience of such groups. This enables individuals who are new to such groups to have peers within the group who are familiar with the PPC format. Where a new group is started from scratch, a small group of five or six relatively high-functioning individuals should be taken first to familiarize themselves with the PPC format, before introducing new members one at a time after a few weeks. Mutual Help Group meetings within the EQUIP framework have five phases:

1. Introduction: the group leader should spend five minutes reflecting on the previous meeting and evaluating the group's progress.
2. Problem reporting: each group member reports any problems they have encountered since the previous meeting. Standard names are used to describe the type of problem it is. This part of the meeting should last around 15 minutes.
3. Awarding the meeting: the group decides which member needs their help the most and awards the meeting to that person. This part of the meeting should take about 5 minutes.

4.   Problem solving: the group try to understand and solve the problems of the member who has been awarded the meeting. This person should then agree to the proposed course of action to solve the problems and to report back to the meeting at set intervals. This part of the meeting should take about 30 minutes.
5.   Summary: the group leader should spend the final five minutes of the meeting summarizing the meeting and what has been accomplished.

Once a positive peer culture has been established the EQUIP programme is started. This consists of the three components in the Anger Replacement Training (ART) programme: skillsstreaming, anger control training and moral reasoning training. These are outlined in *Appendix X*.

The Equipping Peers to Help One Another (EQUIP) programme is available in the following book which includes outlines of the sessions and checklists and problem situations: Gibbs, J. C., Potter, G. B., & Goldstein, A. P. (1995). *The EQUIP Program: Teaching Youth to Think and Act Responsibly Through a Peer-helping Approach*. Champaign, IL: Research Press.